TRINITY STREET

TRINITY STREET

POEMS

JEN CURRIN

ANANSI

Published in Canada in 2023 and the USA in 2023 by House of Anansi Press Inc.
houseofanansi.com

27 26 25 24 23   1 2 3 4 5

Library and Archives Canada Cataloguing in Publication

Title: Trinity Street / Jen Currin.
Names: Currin, Jen, 1972- author.
Description: Poems.
Identifiers: Canadiana (print) 20220445214 | Canadiana (ebook) 20220445230 |
ISBN 9781487011628 (softcover) | ISBN 9781487011635 (EPUB)
Classification: LCC PS8605.U77 T75 2023 | DDC C811/.6—dc23

Book design: Alysia Shewchuk

*House of Anansi Press is grateful for the privilege to work on and create from the Traditional Territory
of many Nations, including the Anishinabeg, the Wendat, and the Haudenosaunee,
as well as the Treaty Lands of the Mississaugas of the Credit.*

Canada Council   Conseil des Arts
for the Arts   du Canada

ONTARIO ARTS COUNCIL
CONSEIL DES ARTS DE L'ONTARIO
an Ontario government agency
un organisme du gouvernement de l'Ontario

With the participation of the Government of Canada
Avec la participation du gouvernement du Canada |

*We acknowledge for their financial support of our publishing program the Canada Council for the Arts,
the Ontario Arts Council, and the Government of Canada.*

Printed and bound in Canada

but god moves to the end
of our sentences

— Robin Blaser

for Karen

Contents

I. The Convention Is Not Over

II. Dear Community

III. Saint in the Rain

IV. Late Prayers

THE CONVENTION IS NOT OVER

From Surrey to Commercial Drive

I was lucky; I caught the bus quickly.

It lurched; I tripped.

My neighbour and I shared an intimacy.

Reading is dangerous; I'd better be ready.

Body an argument; how we are garmented.

Quickly caught the boss: told her two

more books I'd soon finish.

Two more: I had to stop reading.

This poetry lucks me.

Stole an apple from your house

but only to take it to my house

to slice for your breakfast.

A pigeon's wing feathers

my hair as I walk

to the restaurant to meet a friend

who says he wants to take fewer

leaps in his poems, to stick a little

longer with one thing. The leaping

has become too easy.

The bus driver is maybe new, maybe

trying to tame the bus.

It isn't working.

This poetry winks me.

If my fingers hold the pen lightly.

Around a Bend

it takes four months
to fill a notebook

poet's telephone
broken again

with "good" intentions
"I intend"

wasting faith and water

calling witness
for watching TV

you weren't at the protest
that rainy afternoon

your ears infected
with another song

I called you up after
to check your temperature

my boots muddy from the trail

I held hands only
with a tree, whispered to ferns

you lay in bed aching
after painting a brilliant sign

a coyote yipping at your door
rose tea steeping & just like that

we're out of the woods

Poem Beginning and Ending with Lines from Lissa Wolsak

Eternity misfits me

Permanence is the stupidest I have ever

Ideast, I am over

Although the shabby coat

No one ever completes

Even in *The Complete Stories*

The unsteady printer

Years on a sunny shelf you

In the strictest sense, they "lightened"

Some pages are whispers some would like to call you "boyfriend"

It can be said that spirit found

No distinction could keep us together

To visit her house you must

Four jugs needed to boil water

We were advised to carelessly

In a tiny waterfront shack for twenty minutes

Such perceptions—the snort of a horse

An enormous sea lion's snout breaking the surface

What I mean is the intuitive faculty

Someone was fired

"Laid off," someone

Has a little money, not from family

Needs round-the-clock care

Needs a new head scarf

Needs a chance to feel her breasts again

I brought my sacred body and caused it to sit

Gingko Tree

The deaths are often sooner
than expected.
Why?
Did we think
people had unlimited...?
Dip
my toe in weather,
faint up to heaven.

They never guessed the cloud—
scholars waiting.
Raining cold—I quickly mothered
my way out of there,
into friends' apartments
of incense and coffee,
alley views. Awareness
of tenderness, someone's good
luck. Someone gathering
bottles. And now the clanking
of the train.

Friday Mouth

Vocally, from my belly.
From my antlers hang jewels, necklaces
belonging to my grandmothers
and a very large pinecone
my aunt carried around
in a cedar box on her walks.
Witness: here for the ancestors
who call me on creaking phones
in the deep black vitality of night—
I'm sleeping.
Conversations twinkle
the next day, little dusts—
I must make notes.
Reminded again to love
the student who wrote problematic—
What she's trying to work out—
Difficult—
Lungs buck a little
as I bike up the rainy hill
& think of the great American poet in Paris,
compose a letter:
How are you & I heard
another one of your husbands died?
But now's the time to get up
& take some tincture.
Someone I love is leaving
for work & I watch
her slip an earring
into a lobe, lipstick her Friday mouth.
Later I will meet her—
keep my soul in a backpack
so it may be weighed
when I arrive.

Ear, Nose, and Throat

"I need to heal these old woods,"
I texted a friend.
Old wounds
was what I meant.

"Hey cutie" becomes
"Hey cut-throat."
And we wring our hands.

Children come over, make greasy prints
on mirrors and windows,
push all the books
to the back of the shelves.

One child takes out a white volume
called *Snowflake* and sits
down on the floor
to read.

Fog returns, fills the river valley.
A minute ago I could see
the dull buildings—
now they're gone.

We wrap ourselves
in fuzzy robes,
scarves to keep warm.

Late afternoon, sipping
watery coffee, listening
to trains.

A small turquoise pyramid
placed next to the picture
of a garlanded saint.

My only goals
for today are to not turn
on the computer
and to start again
singing.

Where Buildings Pose as Mountains

Just a cape, without a vampire.
A tall woman looking down
into the face of her phone.

The generalizations you like
to make are different
from the generalizations
I like to make.

We "disagree."

Shall we call it a steady rain?

This bright pen hurts my eyes
and the color of this room is unkind,
but the landlord likes it.

If you put your body here, on this chair,
and lift this cup of coffee—what?

Too sober for a proper friendship—
she said it would rain all day.

Some fear instrument they were
always buying/updating.

Where buildings pose as mountains,
their glass aching to be ice.

Yesterday I called it aggression;
today it's the delightfully emphatic way
she has of phrasing things.

I want to walk in the air
where nothing is thinking.

The dimes gathered, lined up
like sand dollars on the mantle.

A friend arrives with masks.
We put them on
and swim through the night.

Dead Phones

some of us love it
when it rains all day

we could even eat lunch
at four

even witness a garden
& taste the metals in the water

anyone can get a cancer
& die or live

to die some other decade
anyone can make a crisp

from foraged blackberries &
windfall apples

on the closest island
we listen to dusk

her radio is always
so exact

the voice kind
as the hand cools

Secretists

just a couple of sharpened pencils
will be enough

& four hours to contemplate
your nasty text

nasty as in mean
not sexy

broken pencils on the floor
like sunlight streaming

moon on fire

I don't want directions
or a "diamond in the rough"

but adrenaline
to give way to

an answer never learned in this life

To Renunciation

Stone. Rain. Apple. Moon.
One side of my body is cold;
the other is fire.

I dress for the door.
A handkerchief, a runny nose.
I dress the body that is cold.

Wait on the steps
of the yoga school
to meet an old teacher.
My knee aches; I don't own a shawl.

She toddles up, wraps
something paisley
around my shoulders.

We never do enter
the school, walk instead
to the hardware store,
buy a baking pan
large enough for
the night's feast.

It's a holiday no one understands.
My people quit
celebrating it years ago.

"Why would you want
the door closed
on the sound of the fountain?"
the teacher asks.

(She is untangling Christmas
lights in the back of the store.)

"The sound of writing water
has always bothered me," I confess.

The teacher laughs
and clicks on the lights.
They pulse around her.

The Convention Is Not Over

they ought not to come here
grab a tissue
turn on a stereo
make a taco

they ought to build up the fire
with some windfall branches
from the recent storm

they ought not to talk (certain) politics

they ought to deviate
illuminate a consciousness
with a lit match

they ought to bring candles, beeswax
& old friends in wrinkled suits
working on labyrinthine story collections

they ought not to make threats
about emotions
or other verbs

it will fall away &
oceans heave

young men & genderqueers
in flouncy floral dresses
smoking as the dawn comes on

Trinity Street

Become later our butter and bread

woke to evening

long lyric written by a drone

small buzz, handheld, last unmodified bee

in the shed, shovels

bag of lime

pruning shears & gloves

the lover of poppies

leaves broccoli seedlings

sat on her stoop last summer

before and after meditation

watered these words

her infinity earrings swinging

she crashed the fence

into a garden holy

with unburdened bodies

DEAR COMMUNITY

Night Train

To drink more coffee, snort
more gingko,
to be able to think
a hard-won thought,
humourless as this
diminishing blue hour,
lustrous as the gold drill
affixed to the giant machine
boring deep into the gravel
across the street
to plant pilings in the marshy soil.

Overhead, a solid steel bank
of cloud, monolithic
as an alien mothership
parked over the river
sending down or blocking
beams of—
Light? Energy? Feeling?

I do not want to look at your face,
dust on the back of a book jacket,
author to fix or finish.
Everything has a language,
she said. If only you'd stop
talking long enough to listen.

Blue—poets like the word
& the color,
even a shell to hold
in front of the eyes
like a magnifying glass.

But to intentionally misunderstand
a prayer—yet who could ever
understand a prayer?

Vestibule—we're waiting
& the night train hurries
us toward our destination.
Steep mountains & a cold
cup of red tea.
Down the corridor
someone has already set our places
at the small round table.
I take up my book,
the lamps flicker on.
With a little brilliance
—or you might call it patience—
these maps might be readjusted.
You smile at me sleepily.
We're just about to arrive.

Periphery

Eating a sandwich on the pier

she is seldom here, dusty
eyebrows of cinnamon
and sunburnt lips.

Taking notes: realist, romantic, romanticist.

Finally the summary: it's summer
and you're okay
with the discomfort,
friends waiting to answer hard questions.

Attach a string of chilies
to the back of your bike.

Bride eating sandwich with fork & knife.

Mind over rooftops,
wind ricocheting through cafe,
buzz of a new coffee grinder.

You asked the evil spirits—
not for advice
but for directions.

They pointed up.

Beggar's Ocean

Always different, a sea
unstacked, dwelling rivery
& death-afraid,
wrapping myself in morning's curtains.

A lamppost bends its head
over a car—are you asleep?

Bewildered each morning
awakening from dreams of red woods,
neighbours who didn't move,
others who open night
like a velvet dress.
We are not the moon
or fog visiting a dead uncle.
The street is a usual place.

Some are lonesome
& sneak out of class early.
Some are loathsome
& why can't we forget their names.
A few of us are glass, just glass.

Death comes even in comical forms,
the crow strutting
the balcony balustrade, stopping
to give you a stare-down.

Hummingbird just for a second—
did she hear our voices?
Sugar-plump, not anxious—
she always moves
at this speed.

A voice on the phone
echoes
underground.

Here in the woods
I am consistently
on fire. Silver
& gold
have I none.

Procure

Those dirty books we managed
to dodge, dusting off
insufficient politics, not
interested in polarizing rhetorics—
poet or politician
scratches an itch
behind ears and I wake
to silverfish digging a canal,
run for hydrogen peroxide
to sizzle it out.
I am made a little
holier with this view
to water, this dress
of dust turned suit
of armour.

My new acquaintance
has written three beautiful books
seemingly in a moment.
I watch them work—
the ink runs out and they write
words in the air that only a few
can read. "All the better,"
I hear a passing elder say
as she boards a downtown train.

Certain of our losses and little else
we trail after,
very inadequately
thinking through a problem
gifted to us by a crow.

I thought Earth was screeching
but she was just speaking
at the volume of fire.

Rhapsodic Trip

We tripped the CEO;

he was late and bruised

to the meeting.

Yet they can't be classified as "terrorists,"

seeing as we never see them

outside a suit or a boardroom

where they detonate suicide belts

and rise in smoke

to form another corporation

out at sea, beyond the spills,

riding to their islands

on oily dolphins.

Here in the city, good company

of thieves and skaters, bicyclists

believing in microbrew.

Someone down the block without a watch

building a stone wall

in the rain

asks the time.

Wake o'clock, brother.

Dear Prince of Melting Icecaps

Bliss has escaped me.

I went down to our beaches.

The oil-sheened, the skinless salmon, the dead

algae, the greasy rocks.

We are in a state. A State.

The moist bliss empty, the air chemical.

The rat on the roof (the political).

The call was internal, societal—

I stood up from a gold chair

in the dank back room of a bank;

you climbed out from under thousands of pennies

piled in a cellar.

We were recently human,

we endeavoured to cycle, we wanted to juggle,

we had only recently learned how to play.

The State blew out our candles

and we were in a gorgeous dark,

directing foot and bike traffic to the bridge.

I have ten headlamps, community,

and you have this hunch

we might get along, get along.

The sea coughs up cellphones

as we build our boats.

A kind rat with a human face helps me

carve the oars.

I vaguely remember

a polar bear's story, the fluff

of myth.

Is it the red sky or the sea?

We hesitate.

Dear Healing Walk

Some believed we were fairies.
It's true we were gay, but we hadn't
yet developed wings.
We had lots of problems and they made us
fly.

We enrolled in Love School.
The classes were very demanding.
And I'm not talking about sex.
Sex was the easy part.

But after we touched, we started
to love, and then there was so much,
piles of homework.

We flew over the Tar Sands.
I saw my cousin in a hazmat suit shovelling gravel.
Another cousin was a dead dummy
guarding a tailing pond—to keep the geese away.

We were bound in prayer, the dead cousin and I.
The living cousin saw it all as a job

until her breast gave way

to cancer.

Then she prayed with us in the form of sugar

poured into a pipeline.

My dead cousin called my cell

with opinions and onion breath.

In the afterlife there is only yesterday.

A scowl where a breast once was.

We biked back to the toxic beach

and took off our clothes.

If you really want to know

we too were already considered dead

but still had a little

patience and six good hours

of sleep.

Six hours in a tent—

waking to cold coffee and ravens,

the lake and the drums—

Dear Clock

Tick-tock.

Riff-raff: my childhood's graph.

My dying mother loans me a book

of terrible stories.

A bouquet of nasturtiums clenched in a fist.

A bouquet of Tar Sands smeared

roses tied to a white cross

next to the highway.

It wasn't cancer, but something just as ordinary.

Siblings huddle under a thin blue blanket.

Family, the first community,

smelling rain in the air.

A hundred bowls of rice set

on a long table

and we are encouraged to crawl

the length of the room.

Germs from the floor touch my lips.

I remember my dead and stubborn mother

and the queen who was above politics.

Maybe it was our class background

but we liked our coffee cold,

our conversations lively.

The air was stale around the thin queen

as she said, "You can enjoy not eating."

This was many years before the death of ice.

Burnt Fortune Cookie

Dress, undress; call, don't call;

forget to text or forget to promise.

Cat playing with a large marble upstairs—

Light to know you by, to try to read by—

Fancy the bright mirrors

you are hanging with your ex-wife.

You found her passport in an old box

of giveaway clothes.

I have stayed up too many nights after night's candle.

Have slept with too many divorcées.

Gotten up too early to write bad sonnets & sip incense.

I have tried to sleep in but have never been attached

enough to "the good life."

Now I must answer "no" to your question

of "What is an individual?"

Launder old unbuttoned pants, plum & full of smoke.

Consider wristwatching & lipsticking—

the machinery all broke up in my mind.

Despite all my critiques, I stayed at your house

where small sentences disturbed the very rooms we tried to sleep in.

I sat down with your family & instead

of blessing the food, they blessed themselves.

Come Together

This historical moment is overwhelming—
you want other people
to be more quiet more often.
On the train, noise
from everyone's phone. Crickets
in cities are just a sad metaphor
for not getting the expected
response from an audience.
Marble floors in a bank
crack but the revolving doors
keep expelling the same face.
It's not our father or for that matter
our mother. Recording the hottest
summer on record again as some late '60s
tune plays from a loft—
we hear it down on the street
and it seems more relevant
now than it did then.
But that's just perspective, I guess,
like the realization that we wasted
autumn in stupid posturing
and positioning and now winter
closes everyone's windows
and the songs are sealed up inside.

Journalists Arrive in Cadillacs

everyone's lighting French cigarettes

heaven is a five-star boutique
with shattered windows—
the dresses are ours

the honeyed rooms
the mystic buzzing

high school dropouts
we were sometimes hinting

filled up with ruin
empty boots in the rain

we were sometimes moth-lit, moon

workers in a bookstore
before we forged a union

our knees injured
our crackling dances

our fires
our barely controlled
flames

Dear Community

I'm not sure of the temperature,
the timid nature of these words.

Accepting your feedback—
it hurts
& it's good enough.
I'll take it.

Ten hours of rain sounds
from a YouTube video.

The noise of the city, pile-driving
& grinding like teeth in the night.

Lemon juice & water, sipping clumps of pith.

You think plump yeast, rosemary and olive bread.
I think dry dry cracker.

That dust over there? That's us.

I assume you brought your phone
with you to New York
& I assume you'll bring me.

A little piece of vitamin flashback—
I remember that super moon,
I remember how loosely we danced.

Fish are asking for another life—

Very earnest, these symptoms
born from a system
built of paper & tired blood.

Similar qualities
shared on a blanket
underneath a reaching magnolia
flowering pink & white & pink
&—
one more question?

Are we still in the same poem?

I am waiting for you in all of these rooms.

SAINT IN THE RAIN

Saint in the Rain

But why meditation?
Why something in my eye?
"In all wisdom traditions
there is a state
of consciousness..."

The saint took a sip, then threw
the cup of coffee away.
"I am walking with you," she said,
"to where they are
trying the pipelines.
I have something for the men
stuffed in money shirts,
choking on their ties.
Let us go."

And so we went, following
after her
and now each step
begins
in
reverence.

Brackets

I had two sisters.
Parentheses.
I had a brother, I believed I had
myself.
After guitar lessons, laughter.
After gender lessons, shame.
Every shirt fit us both.
I wanted to be both.
The label said wash with like
colours in cold water.
The music teacher at recital
said where is your dress.
Flutes and clarinets
broke in my hands.
A reason to read was freedom.
A way out of that mouldy house.
Whenever a board fell
I was responsible. Whenever a spider
visited, bites festered.
One by one, we drew
an imaginary plant
and climbed it into the clouds.

In the Cold

You have another imaginary conversation. Someone tells you to shut up and you listen. This is December and these are ethical preferences. Not a day for walking—heel rubbed raw in awkward boots, dusk at 3 p.m. Unrelenting rain dampens the new collection of an old friend's poetry. Every time you dip your hand into your bag, a book cuts you. She climbed onto the off-ramp and lay down, just three years and a month after her mother stepped quickly from a bridge, left the car running, door wide open. The last time you saw them together they were drinking soda and vodka, no limes.

You pray she was high when she left. You pray she was high when she left. You pray. You pray. You pray.

Clockwork

The bathroom smells
like musty old towels
& sweaty jogging bras.
I don't know why
I find this comforting.
Maybe because I grew up
in a mildewy house
& every old drunk
is my mother just as
when you were a child
every bearded man
was your father.

Someone who loved the burning
of holy wood
came to our house
but I don't remember who.

John, or some other
handsome bear of a man?

A February dance,
mystics & whirligigs—
someone saw a chaste cat
on a windowsill
& chased it.

Someone was over
& we made coffee
& mistakes.
We made
a lot of mistakes.

That time I caught
the wrong train
in a rainy, post-sex haze.
We had fucked,
then fought.

You showed me
your turquoise toenails
in the bath
& for some reason
this made me *furious*.

Growing up they
would have called this
conceited
& we're not yet
humility maybe
I was humming
under our breath.

Out of an Envelope

Beautiful blue teeth,
this music.
How many pieces
of my fiddle? How many
black, red, chartreuse olives?
I should be leaving
in an hour but better to stay
here and remedy
this deficiency, flush
down the toilet
the medication that made
my daughter feel numb.
The peppermint soap
she washes her hands
and hair with—soaks
her scarf after
it's been dragged
on the ground. The apartment
surrounded by foggy
mountains, a tugboat
pulling a barge
of squashed cars.
She is the intelligence
handing me gentle papers
and shooing away
a weird moth.
"That could be your
grandmother," I say,
unfolding one of the sheets.
Music notes—a song
composed
during her most recent

bout of insomnia.
Headached all day
and neither of us
stomached a painkiller.
This room is not broken,
except for that table
which used to be "mine."
There is a stain on it
that looks like wine dissolving.

Gardenia

Erotica and don't want to be in touch anymore. Street listen and whisper. When he came out of the curtain he was a man, and when he stepped back, a woman. I fixed her hair all night.

Alkaline Water

They think it makes sense.
They think incense.
In case
a random package—
my lost luggage,
let's just call it my father's
body floating in the purple
seas of heaven.

And it's difficult, this
plagiarism. We can't
just open a book
and copy a page.
We have to *listen*.

Before we steal,
we wait and shake.
We have a few
nuclear codes
in our pockets
in a seriously way.

We might sit around
in our underwear
reading interviews.

People still get famous—
at any age.

I have a big stack
of event tickets
on my shelf.

I want to give one to you
in the most seriously
way but I fear
like an October avocado
it is rotten
in the middle.

I'm not entirely sure
how depression works.
I'm not a doctor.

We were created
in this world
and ginger and turmeric
are just part
of the lyric
that just now
has no laughter
in it.

Our fear of occult experiences
as we prep
another little pill.

In Orange

I came to your house to carry the cake to the car, to drive the car to the friend's apartment, to lift the cake to the roof, to unhook the glasses from the cupboard, to uncork the wine on the table, to laugh at untold jokes, to watch the skyline swallow the fog, to slip a message into the claw of a pigeon, a pigeon you carried into our house, calling her Cake. My friend was not yet ghost; by ten she would be. By twelve the next day my sister called. And before she said "news," I heard the news in her voice. She didn't have a cold. She had once had a friend who baked us lemon cake, careful cursive "happy birthday" in orange. I never understood how, coming from her family, she could be so kind. I understand now I never thanked her. Now she scares me in photos held up at night.

Mixed Tulip Bouquet

Ghost competitors dwell
shoving & moaning.
So-called days pass,
falling petals of cherry
lighten asphalt.
We bike over
breathing forsythia & hyacinth,
plotting a melody as it reverberates
a passing car.
Green has started talking
on trees bare just last week.
A lioness entered the room
& fell asleep.
Second week of April she yawns,
stretches & pads away.

"Little scoundrels," our teacher
was fond of saying, taking
off her black watch
to slap our cheeks
gently. It's something we remember
every time we touch
a vibrating belly, try to
sing through makeshift barricades.

She said poets can say things
like that, like, "We're all going to die."
Fiction writers have to be more subtle
or was it careful,
was that what she said?

In the garden stung by fairy lights
drinking ruby and golden ales
listening to poets descant
& fiction button up its fury
in clever stories.

Someone wasn't wearing underwear
when her period started
& there was a wad
of toilet paper to fix that.

Someone took off her bra
& proffered it, fuchsia & lace,
disappointingly
too large.

We were all in the dark.
A certain monster was listening
so we turned off our phones.

A Shadow's Cat

Lamp clicks on in a dark room.
The apartment throbs with light.
Tonight I must dream.
Three nights of bad sleep.
Wait for a friend to call/email/text.
Wait for a friend to lie about drinking.
Rise at 3 a.m. like a shadow's cat,
slip down to the boiler room,
turn up the heat.
When we see our breath
indoors we know
we are breathing.
Unfamiliar again to myself
as dawn climbs the buildings.

Bells

With a laugh like that. With a laugh like that how could you. With kids like that. Two kids like that. With hair like that. Midnight gleam like that. Thrift store lace leggings, stylish nip-and-tuck dresses. Handmade chocolates rolled in coconut and slivered almonds. When we sniffed from baggies in downtown bathroom stalls. Peach coolers before nightfall. Dancing underage, hitching back to the boards of a falling-apart house. It was rented, of course. A rental. The rooms you made so inexpensively beautiful. Paisley shawl tossed over hand-me-down couch, a glass slipper never worn by your grandmother. Before the cutting. Before the clutches. You drew pictures of our future selves. Worked at a shoe store, a convenience store, a golf course, another greasy kitchen. Dial-up sex. Trash can of empty bottles. You couldn't make it beautiful. How could you. The voices rising. Snake tightening around your neck. With a laugh like that. Like that the bridge was always waiting.

January 4

Salt and pepper the noose.
Hungry tonight.
From stone to aloe. From salmon.
Here now, on two legs, talking.
Walking into the probiotic dawn,
holding out a hand to the healer
with an infection. Ear. Heart. Either.
Definitely later, special and residual,
with the joy of eels.
For years I lived in that corner
with the tender spider
until my young nephew
taught me how to send a blessing:
"It's easy. You just think
of someone.
Then you think of them
smiling."

LATE PRAYERS

Micro-dose

I am writing an article about mushrooms
for a magazine that pays in craft beer.

They poached ginseng from the woods—
left the patch in shambles.

I haven't been studying my French
and I've forgotten the word for "reverence."

The cities dwindle
but the mysteries have never gone away.

On a hill, high as cats
who licked the acid-bowl.

Sacred fern, smallest Garry oak,
fallen cedar drilled open by two red-headed woodpeckers.

I rocked in a cold breath
on the bathroom floor.

The holy man kept a tiger as a pet,
healed the villagers with hands-on ginger and turmeric.

LSD five times and Molly just twice.
I decided to major in accounting.

A micro-dose with coffee to stave off
the predations of depressive thoughts.

My mother kept the peyote in her top drawer
and in July finally flushed it down the toilet.

My father took LSD and lost his virginity
on a hayride.

Some of my friends have a high education.
Some of my friends never take a sip.

She wants to walk to the river later.
I want to walk on the river later.

I never tell anyone where I worship,
why, or how.

Let the Candidate Fill Her Mind

When I was a diplomat—wait—I
was never a diplomat, my letters
explosive, inexpert & herb-drenched.

They gave me back my cumin
& cancelled the reading,
told me,
"Sip a peppermint tea, or hibiscus."

But her dangling turquoise bird earrings—
every rose tree—
every dove perched on chimney's corner—

And jasmine tea bag,
torn-up schoolbag.

Whenever I sit with them
(which is often)
I leave a few coins
in the donation box.

The monks don't mind
the money
or seem to mind
my breath—
constant companion
until I leave this life.

Salad for Two

This is a deck of cards
for non-believers just like you.
For stationery typers
& architects who dance
while drawing.
Someone is a mouse or wants
to make a famous poem.
A mousy poem, a little bit like
your cousin with that colour of hair.
Someone was born a mouse
& grew up to be a rat.
Now she lives in the moon,
chews it every day.
Aghast you should suggest
she's a ghost—& why
you need death
to feel empathy.
Feel anything—sand
in the lettuce, string of celery
between your teeth.
A bewildering rage,
a list of flower seeds you hope to buy.
A little arrow of bad thought
is sent out to the president.
Can't snatch it back.
Next week my letter will be better.

Ascension Academy

She makes whole schools
out of paper & dust,
ink & intention.
A violin healer,
she is my dearest long-time friend.
We sip green tea-infused gin,
snack on spicy vegan cheeses.
We were at that party
last week, talking New Orleans,
offices of the inner circle
of a guru we both claim to know.
Bought each other hardcover
books for Christmas
& read some words channelled
by Christ. "He was more
well-received than official
history would have us
believe," my friend reveals,
a bit of ashy cheese
balanced on the tip of her finger.
She is densifying the calcium
in her bones through sheer
force of will. Looking
into her green eyes
I have to admit again
she is not aging.

Makers of Silver and Gold

I can't believe a saint
once rode a train
up the coast from Portland
to Vancouver. She stayed
in this very hotel, downtown,
for two whole nights.

Years later, I sleep
on her starched pillow
and roses distress my dreams.

Personality—I'm suspicious of it.
I have one, of course,
several actually, but
isn't it/aren't they
just a container
from which ego-yogurt
too easily slips?
I like probiotics, I know
they're good for me, wheat germ
and chia seeds, and you,
you are too, the friend
who is constantly in a state
of self-created emergency.
Even through avoidance
and dislike
you teach me.

If only the saint
would visit now
while we are still middle-aged
and marginally alive.

But she was eighty years ago.
Always fond of dawn departures,
she left by mail train,
crossed the continent,
and got on a boat to Europe,
leaving us standing in fields
of soy, corn, and wheat
with our palms turned
toward the mottled sky.

The horsey laugh of my friend
I miss, and I think of recommending
a mug of mood-balancing tea,
a podcast hosted by a calm-voiced
Zen-lover.

Instead, another friend
who has given up capital
for fog filling a river valley
texts to say, don't promise,
don't perish on the ferry
back to the suburbs.

I remember people who are
more solitary,
their particular happinesses.

I haven't let anyone down.

Near the Orchard

I'm not very good at following
directions — have you noticed?
How often I'm like an inch
of cold green tea in a chipped
mug? The blue one
borrowed when we carried boxes
into your new communal house,
pots of rosemary and sage on the front steps.
I'm sorry I haven't given it back yet
but I want to tell you about
this cave, very dark
except for the veins of gold
running through the ceiling. A cave
I've spent some time in
and you are now arching
your foot toward,
holding an old record player.
The song has to be listened to
alone — we both know that.
You'll go into the cave and call it
"community work."
I'll lend you hand salve, a lamp,
earplugs if you need them.
You will say better
to have the airline vouchers
expire than to have taken
this trip.
You smell rain
sinking into mud,
you smell rain splashing
on Chinook territory,
Portland pavement. You think

of safety, imagine sun slanting
through bay windows as your mother
puts on another hippie album
so the children can dance.
I've learned there are a few things
I can't live without:
coffee, books, my body.
And friendship, it turns out.

Dawn

The elevator broke down
on the seventh floor
and we walked a long green hallway
of locked closets.
My mother was a janitor
and later a secretary and even
later a mail carrier and at twelve
I took my brother's dirt bike,
just started delivering papers.
She told the doctor about her dream,
elevator sinking to the lowest red floors,
and he got scared, got the shivers.
It was a full moon payday,
which is to say a very violent Friday.
Sores on her lips hadn't healed
when we wheeled her back
to the retirement home's lobby.
She asked, "When was the last
time *you* walked on the moon?"
And told us tonight a disco
in the rec room,
music of an elevator
sped up and glittering.
Mother reminds: a little grandiose
storytelling never hurt
nobody. To think
where an elevator takes us.

The Local

"Poetry is local," my friend from St. Paul
once told me. I was living
in Portland at the time, rising
at 5 a.m. for a coffee shop job.
Didn't know if I knew any Multnomah people
but there were always so many strangers,
workers to share silence with
on the pre-dawn bus. The chill
in the air, February,
what frost smelled like,
bending close to an iced windshield.
To be young and type lines
on a discarded typewriter in my brother's
dim room was my late
afternoon occupation. I never
went to bed early enough
and abhorred toast,
all breakfast foods.
My boss made one strangely
benign innuendo. Power:
I knew I was sexier,
knew my allusions
to the previous night's antics
kept the customers entertained.
People often asked if I was
a native of that city.
I've always hated that expression.

Twins

After creating the sun with some fire and an axe,
she used an old notebook
to contact her dead brother.
He hadn't yet called
from any of his other worlds.
He stumbled out of this one
while his body stayed by the river.
Why the book of someone
could never be burnt
she couldn't quite figure.
A dip in the river, flower
shutting its eyes
to sleep. A long song,
soft vocals still playing
on headphones left on a rock.
"This book is politically important,"
she said, although it seemed
she might try to drown it
or axe it to pieces.
A brother goes into a cave
and never comes out.
Even though she cannot draw
this, cannot enter the chaos
or attend a class on making amends,
she extends
and he is there, just on the other side
of the veil,
waiting in a world they once
woke in, side by side, bare feet,
unconcerned sandals,
a dip of water from the well
a small sip before
they ran off to play.

The Woods

She told me she was going
into the woods
to find the divine feminine.
"I will be holding onto her skirts
even if I'm dragged
through the mud," she wrote
on a postcard bearing a picture
of a northern flicker.

 She instructed young people
on how to be self-sufficient.
"That's a black bear. Back away."
"That cave of throbbing
light is what we came for—
but don't go inside
just yet."

The coral lipstick she wore
on our second date
stained my white shirt.
We met—like so many—
online. I was surprised
by her agile fingers. After a while
we lost touch: I stewed
in loneliness, she fell in love
with her straight roommate,
writing her voluminous notes
swaddled in pink envelopes
which she slid under her door.
That was the year I finished college
just as the great experimental composer
died, and although I wasn't invited

I wondered what cake, what
prayer at their wedding.

.

.

Handkerchief

"The tiger yogi
who can sit
with a tiger—
some call her Mother.
Now *that's* a new year."

I had wondered
when we would
get to
renunciation.

All this sadness
comes from the shock
of loss.

I interviewed scholars
for eight hours,
studied very intensely
death
and all its surroundings.

When my aunt died
I delved further
into impermanence
by moving in
with a renunciate
in a suburban cave.

She chided me daily
about my mild addictions.
There was no coffee;
my head always hurt.

She talked a quiet life
of eating vegetables
but kept all the sugar
for herself.

I was lucky all the same.
My sadness slowly widened.
I started a radio show
broadcast from a friend's boat
called (I think) *Lucid
Experience.*

It was all volunteer
and we had never been so happy.

I Assume the Poets Will Continue at Their Trade

Two friends leave dead marriages.

It's January already; the president is dead.

Believe the leaves.

They're coming back.

You beg a beginning.

You say I never play my guitar.

You say I don't own a guitar.

You say I don't own you.

Notebook testament.

She used to stretch

her fingers before playing.

There can be a lot to read

& worry about if that's how

you want to start your morning.

My fingers are very out of practice.

"My" president has not yet

been elected.

She is under the sludge

in the Stó:lō River, waiting

to wake

us up.

Incarnate

They were intimidated
by poets who were
as good as them.
"Love's flaccid," I heard
at the bar. Or believed
I did. Folks who know
"the unknown."
Or thought they did.
A person named Rainbow
who used to sit with us
at the Zen center
always had the best advice—
by which I mean they never
gave any, but one time
encouraged us to volunteer
for the annual homeless count.
"The population has doubled
in ten years," they told us.
Another time they were surprisingly
unfazed by the planet's impending death
while others in the circle cried.

These are the discussions

I remember

that came after the silence.

Late to Work and Listening

to another podcast about the hugging
saint. Some people
are very devotional—
they have a whole room
dedicated, they stretch
and pray every day.

If I stew in gratitude,
sipping tea only a whisper away
from hot water,
other parts of me turn in small graves,
thinking of all the things
they want/want not to change.
Forests seen from a suburban bus,
a powerful squat
my lover showed me,
an island just to the south
of where I temporarily live, in the middle
of a river that hasn't yet
been taken or given back. Salmon
swim upstream
and will we eventually?

I asked this as the saint
was smiling, silently packing
my bags.

Salt Water

In every envy article why does the speaker
feel powerful

A suggestion of butter on toast, catching
the early bus

The belief that social media might
save us

That we might die after playing
dead

Her memory is incredibly bad—that's how
she survives

Wake up & walk down to the corner store where
milk curdles

Every archive's lost envelope contains
this calculation

You pinch me & remind, math is not
for poets

Neither is poetry
I agree

We laugh before the joke
is finished

Where Is the Water in this Story

They weren't very good emcees,
talking about pistols, lavender
& last call.

I had joined their cult
to disappear
& instead
they gave me their gold-plated
deity.

She said we're not finished yet.
No, no—these deities aren't done
yet.

Any choir might remember
forgiving a song

& those mean men out back
burying another canister
of cold silver.

I kept thinking the lyrics
would get better—
that we'd all catch
fire in our chests,

shake out coins from pockets
while changing clothes.

But she was pissed.
You can't trick
a clairvoyant.

Talking about "you women" —
she meant the men —
& those of us "in between."

She was serious, dishing up glasses
of cayenne water
to clear out the bugs
crowding our intestines,

each of her words
a weightless
orange.

She suggested
the disruption
would be very interesting
or at the very least
possibly
healing.

Acknowledgements and Notes

This book was written on the traditional, ancestral, and unceded territories of the Qayqayt, Kwantlen, Kwikwetlem, Musqueam, Squamish, and Tsleil-Waututh Nations.

Thanks to the editors and readers of the following publications, in which some of these poems have previously appeared, sometimes in different versions: *Arc, Ambit, Canadian Literature, The Elephants, filling Station, Grain, Hamilton Review of Arts and Letters, The Headlight Review, Pageboy, Poetry Northwest, River City Poetry, Timberline Review, Trampoline,* and *Watch Your Head: Writers and Artists Respond to the Climate Crisis.* Thank you to the 2018 Alberta Magazine Awards for awarding a Silver Award in Poetry to "Dear Healing Walk" and "Rhapsodic Trip."

Deep gratitude to my editor, Kevin Connolly, for the best editing advice and a very astute eye. Thank you to Christine Leclerc and Karen Smith for feedback on a couple of these poems.

Thank you to Wade Comer for letting me use his beautiful photograph for the cover, and thank you to Alysia Shewchuk for the design. Gratitude to all of the other folks at House of Anansi for their work on this book, including Leigh Nash, Karen Brochu, Michelle MacAleese, Laura Chapnick,

Ricky Lima, Nicole Lambe, Lucia Kim, Debby de Groot, Emma Rhodes, and Leslie Joy Ahenda. Thank you to Emmett Race/Sarah Race Photography for author photos over the years.

The Robin Blaser epigraph is from "Image-Nation 5 (erasure." Many thanks to Soma Feldmar for locating the title when I couldn't. The two lines in "Poem Beginning and Ending with Lines from Lissa Wolsak" are from *Pen Chants: Or Nth or 12 Spirit-Like Impermanences.* Thank you to Lissa for her important work. Gratitude to Erin Robinsong for her poem "Late Prayer," from which the last section takes its title, and thank you to Susan Steudel for sending me the poem. Thanks to Cole Nowicki for the silverfish story.

Kazim Ali and Mercedes Eng: thank you, thank you, thank you for making time to say some thoughtful words about this collection.

Deep bows to all of my writer-pals for their kindnesses, for the communities we share. Endless thanks to my friends and family for their love and support. A special thank you to my beloved Karen, for everything.

Thanks to the Canada Council for the Arts for a grant that gave me time to work on this collection.

"From Surrey to Commercial Drive" is dedicated to Raoul, "In the Cold" is dedicated to Becky, "Friday Mouth" is dedicated to Karen.

"Dear Healing Walk": The Tar Sands Healing Walk was an event that took place annually from 2009 to -2014 to draw attention to the destruction and pollution of Athabascan lands as a result of Alberta's Tar Sands. The Healing Walk was founded by a coalition of women from Indigenous communities impacted by Tar Sands projects. Later, they were assisted by Keepers of the Athabasca, a network of Indigenous, Métis, and settler community members along the Athabasca River. I attended the final Healing Walk in 2014, where I was a guest on the territories of the five local First Nations comprising the Athabasca Tribal Council (Athabasca Chipewyan First Nation, Fort McKay First Nation, Chipewyan Prairie First Nation, Fort McMurray First Nation, and Mikisew Cree First Nation) and the Métis Nation. My gratitude to the founders and organizers of the Tar Sands Healing Walk, and the nations who hosted us on the shores of Willow Lake. May the Healing Walk's slogan, "Stop the Destruction. Start the Healing," become a lived reality.

JEN CURRIN lives on unceded Qayqayt, Kwantlen, Kwikwetlem, and Musqueam territories (New Westminster, BC) and teaches writing at Kwantlen Polytechnic University. Jen's first collection of stories, *Hider/Seeker*, was awarded a Canadian Independent Book Award and was named a 2018 *Globe and Mail* Best Book. They have published four previous collections of poetry, *The Sleep of Four Cities*, *Hagiography*, *The Inquisition Yours* (winner of the 2011 Audre Lorde Award), and *School*.